Popcorn

World War One

Stephen White-Thomson

WAYLAND

Explore the world with **Popcorn** - your complete first non-fiction library.

Look out for more titles in the Popcorn range. All books have the same format of simple text and striking images. Text is carefully matched to the pictures to help readers to identify and understand key vocabulary. www.waylandbooks.co.uk/popcorn

Published in paperback in 2014 by Wayland
Copyright © Wayland 2014

Wayland
Hachette Children's Books
338 Euston Road
London NW1 3BH

Wayland Australia
Level 17/207 Kent Street
Sydney NSW 2000

 Produced for Wayland by
White-Thomson Publishing Ltd
www.wtpub.co.uk
+44 (0)843 208 7460

All rights reserved.
Editor: Stephen White-Thomson
Designer: Clare Nicholas
Picture researcher: Stephen White-Thomson
Series consultant: Kate Ruttle
Design concept: Paul Cherrill

British Library Cataloguing in Publication Data
White-Thomson, Stephen.
   World War I. -- (History corner)(Popcorn)
   1. World War, 1914-1918--Juvenile literature.
   I. Title II. Series
   940.4-dc23

ISBN: 978 0 7502 8385 4

Wayland is a division of Hachette Children's Books,
an Hachette UK company.
www.hachette.co.uk

Printed and bound in China

10 9 8 7 6 5 4 3 2 1

Picture/illustration credits:
Corbis: Hulton-Deutsch Collection 4-5, 13, 14,
Swim Ink 2, LLC/Corbis 6, 7, 18, Corbis 15; Kobal:
Dreamworks SKG/The Kobal Collection 18; Mary
Evans: Mary Evans/Robert Hunt Collection 16;
Shutterstock: Vaughan Sam title page and 9, cycreation
imprint page and 20, Willem Havenaar 20-21; Topfoto:
ullsteinbild/Topfoto 8, The Granger Collection cover
and 10, The World History Archive/Topfoto 11; Peter
Bull Illustration 23

Every effort has been made to clear copyright.
Should there be any inadvertent omission,
please apply to the publisher for rectification.

Contents

World at war

World War One was called a world war because so many countries joined in. It lasted four years, between 1914 and 1918.

More than 65 million men from 30 countries fought in the war.

Countries like Britain, France and Russia were on one side. We call them the Allies. The main country on the other side was Germany.

Millions of soldiers were killed during the war.

Joining up

At first, men were excited to join the army. They wanted to help their country win the war. They thought they would win in a few months.

This poster asks men to join the army.

COME AND DO YOUR BIT

JOIN NOW

The soldiers had to leave their homes. They had to say goodbye to their families and friends and go off to fight tough battles. Many never came back.

In this poster, women tell their husbands to go and fight.

Digging in

The soldiers dug deep ditches called trenches.
These were to protect them from gunfire.
Men lived in the trenches for many weeks.
They ate meals and slept in the trenches.

A British soldier keeps guard in a
trench while other soldiers sleep.

It was often muddy, wet and cold in the trenches. Rats stole the food. Soldiers on both sides were often bombed and shot at.

This trench has been kept so we can see what trenches looked like during the war.

Trench warfare

Often, the soldiers had to leave their trenches and attack the other side. This was called 'going over the top'.

This painting shows men 'going over the top' in the middle of winter.

The land between trenches was called 'no man's land'. Soldiers had to run across it to attack the enemy. It was very dangerous.

The trenches stretched for 725 kilometres.

Soldiers carry a wounded man to safety.

Women and war

Women could not join the army. At home, they did jobs men normally did. They worked in factories that made bombs.

Women mend a road on a London street.

Women looked after injured soldiers in hospital. Many women worked on farms to grow food to feed all the people at home.

This poster asks women to join the Women's Land Army.

By 1917, 260,000 women were working on farms.

NATIONAL SERVICE
WOMEN'S LAND ARMY

"GOD SPEED THE PLOUGH AND THE WOMAN WHO DRIVES IT"

SERIES W9.
APPLY FOR ENROLMENT FORMS AT YOUR NEAREST POST OFFICE OR EMPLOYMENT EXCHANGE

The home front

People at home still went hungry. They had to grow as much of their food as possible.

Parks in towns were turned into giant vegetable gardens.

Hungry children queue up to get soup from a 'soup kitchen'.

Families had to be careful what they ate. They weren't allowed to eat too much. The soldiers needed to be well fed so they could keep fighting.

A poster tells people at home not to waste food.

FEED a FIGHTER
Eat only what you need –
Waste nothing –
That he and his family
may have enough

Animals in the war

Animals were used in the war in many different ways. Dogs pulled machine guns and carried messages. Pigeons also carried messages between the trenches.

A soldier writes a message for a dog to carry.

The book and film *War Horse* tells the story of two horses. Horses were used to pull heavy guns. Many horses died in the war.

This poster is for the film *War Horse*.

The war ends

In 1917, America joined the war. The Americans had a big army and new weapons. Finally, the Allies defeated the Germans.

An American poster shows soldiers 'going over the top.'

At 11 o'clock on 11 November 1918, the fighting stopped. Everyone was happy the war had ended, but sad that so many people had been killed.

People danced in the streets when they heard the war was over.

Remembering

Remembrance Day is on 11 November each year. On this day, people think about all the soldiers who have died in wars.

Remembrance Day is sometimes called 'Poppy Day'.

REMEMBRANCE DAY
LEST WE FORGET

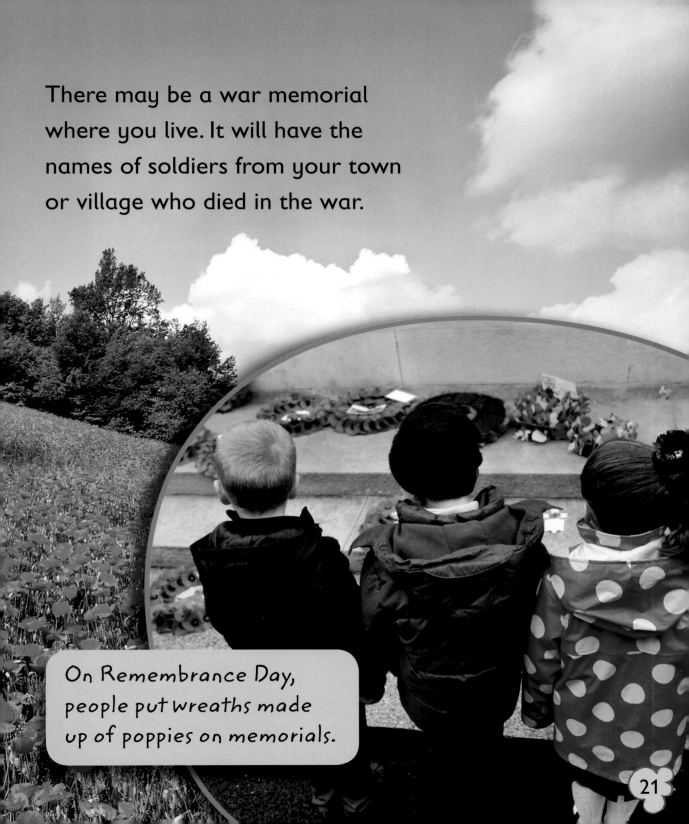

There may be a war memorial where you live. It will have the names of soldiers from your town or village who died in the war.

On Remembrance Day, people put wreaths made up of poppies on memorials.

21

World War One quiz

What have you found out about World War One?
Can you match the words in the panel with the
sentences below?

> a. Allies   b. 'going over the top'   c. no man's land
>
> d. *War Horse*   e. Remembrance Day   f. trench

1. I'm a long hole dug in the ground where it was safer
    to stay during fighting.

2. I'm the area of ground between two trenches.

3. I'm a film made about animals in World War One.

4. I'm the day when we remember people who have died
    in wars.

5. I'm the group of countries that joined together to fight
    the enemy.

6. I'm the name given to the moment when soldiers left
    their own trenches to attack the enemy trenches.

Answers: 1=f, 2=c, 3=d, 4=e 5=a, 6=b.

Make a poppy

You will need:
- a £2 coin and a £1 coin
- red paper • black paper
- a green pipe cleaner
- glue • scissors
- sticky tape

Many of the battlefields of World War One are now farmland. The fields are often covered with poppies. Wear your poppy on Remembrance Day. Ask an adult if you can use the coins to buy a poppy too.

1. Draw round the £2 coin four times on the red paper. Cut out the circles. Draw round the £1 coin once on the black paper. Cut out the circle.

2. Glue the red circles together so they overlap. Glue the black circle in the middle of the red circles on the front.

3. Turn your poppy over. Use sticky tape to fix the pipe cleaner to the back of the poppy. This makes a stalk.

Glossary

army large group of people who are trained to fight on land in a war

bomb weapon that explodes and hurts people or damages things

gunfire when lots of guns shoot many bullets quickly

home front people who stay at home during a war and how they live

machine gun weapon that quickly fires many bullets from a metal tube

soldier someone who is a member of an army

soup kitchen place where free or cheap food is served

trenches holes dug into the ground where soldiers can hide

war memorial something that is built to remember soldiers who have died in wars

weapon something that a person can use to hurt or kill someone

wounded to be hurt

wreath circle of flowers or leaves twisted together

Index